YOGA

for a healthy heart

YOGA
for a healthy heart

BIJOYLAXMI HOTA

RUPA
PUBLICATIONS INDIA

Text Copyright © Bijoylaxmi Hota 2006
E-mail: bijoyhota@rediffmail.com

First Published 2006
Third Impression 2012

Published by
Rupa Publications India Pvt. Ltd.
7/16, Ansari Road, Daryaganj,
New Delhi 110 002

Sales Centres:

Allahabad Bengaluru Chennai
Hyderabad Jaipur Kathmandu
Kolkata Mumbai

Printed in India by
Nutech Photolithographers
B-240, Okhla Industrial Area, Phase-I,
New Delhi 110 020, India

Thanks to
Swami Swaroopananda (Bhubaneswar)
Dr. Pramod Kumar Misra, Dr. Ram Manohar Lohia Hospital, New Delhi

Designed and illustrated by
Ishtihaar

*With the blessings
of my Guru and Guide*

Paramahamsa Swami Satyananda Saraswati

Contents

CHAPTER ONE

Accepting the Amazing Alternative

Long ago when I first began treating ailments with yoga, my teacher warned me against taking heart patients. He had said, that should a patient have a heart attack after joining my class and before yoga could have its effects, yoga would be held responsible and I would acquire a negative reputation. Realising the sense behind his suggestion, I stayed away from heart patients for many years.

Then a close friend developed hypertension, with her blood pressure elevated she required immediate medication. Knowing fully well the ill effects of anti-hypertensive drugs, I could not allow her to take them for long. I therefore had no choice but to treat her.

9

I began by teaching her some prescribed yogic techniques in the usual manner, but that did not yield satisfactory results. Her blood pressure remained high. I took out all my books on yoga and other healing methods, studied them thoroughly again, and meditated intensely. At last I hit upon a yogic routine that normalised her blood pressure in just three days. Encouraged, I began treating others. Each patient had the same result, though not always in three days. However, the results never took longer than ten to fifteen days, and most patients normalised their blood pressure within a week.

Yoga's quick effect on such a serious problem as high blood pressure, which is branded by medical science as incurable, takes many of my patients by surprise. I remember a renowned journalist who came to me with this problem. On the third day of treatment, when his blood pressure measured normal for the first time in twenty five years, he could not believe the results and thought, it had to be a fluke. The next day his blood pressure was even lower and the gentleman was quite puzzled, but he still did not believe that yoga had not only stabilised his blood pressure but had normalised it. The next day, when his pressure dropped even lower, he had no choice but to accept yoga's efficacy.

On the other hand not believing in yoga's quick effects can land the practitioner in dire trouble. Mr. Singh, a former top bureaucrat, came to me for treatment. As usual, I explained that with yoga the blood pressure could drop quickly, so he should monitor his pressure every day during the treatment period to avoid unpleasant consequences. He did not believe me and hence did not bother to check. On the third day, his wife called to cancel the class, saying her husband was feeling very low. I enquired about his blood pressure, which of course they had not checked. I advised her to do so immediately. The next day, when he was not feeling better, they sent for a doctor. When the doctor checked his blood pressure, it was 90/60. This man had continued to take his anti-hypertensive drugs and in the meantime his blood pressure had become normal. The drugs caused his pressure to drop below normal. If he had continued this for a few more days it could have been dangerous.

Normalising simple high blood pressure is faster and easier than normalising hypertension accompanied by other ailments, such as diabetes and asthma. One of my patients had asthma and high blood pressure. When she took medicine for asthma, her blood pressure rose to a dangerous level; yet she could not manage without the asthma medicines. This meant that unless her asthma was cured, her blood pressure would not normalise. And yogic treatment for asthma calls for practices that are contra-indicated for high blood pressure. The same is true with diabetes and cardiovascular problems. But I was amazed when this simple treatment for high blood pressure was enough to

control her condition. After she took up yoga, her asthma became manageable and no longer required medication.

The advice of a competent medical practitioner is essential during the treatment period as per the regimen in this book. More so, for the withdrawal of medicines. When my friend's beta-blocker medication had to be withdrawn, her physician refused to do so. We asked a few more doctors, but no one was willing to help us. I then remembered a doctor patient of mine whose blood pressure had been normalised with yoga. I called him and explained the situation. He agreed to come and see my friend, but never came and would not return my phone calls. I was in a soup; my friend's pulse had slowed down to forty something. Either her medication or her yoga had to be stopped—and soon. She and I chose to stop the medication. My intuition and experience proved right; everything went smoothly and her blood pressure remained normal.

However, before starting yoga for high blood pressure, I advise you to find a doctor who is truly open minded. Some doctors say they believe in yoga, but it may be mere lip service. Once during a conversation with a senior cardiologist in the famed AIIMS, I mentioned the success rate of yoga on high blood pressure. Though a believer in yoga, he was most skeptical regarding this. He claimed that even Dr. Deepak Chopra, who was a student of his, admitted that high blood pressure could not be cured through yoga and meditation. Not to be deterred, I offered to treat twenty of his patients and prove my claim, but to no avail. He would not give me a chance.

Anti-hypertensive medicines must be tapered off gradually, with blood pressure readings checked at least daily. One patient stopped taking the medicines suddenly and his blood pressure shot up to an abnormal high before yoga had time to take effect. Also, you should check your blood pressure regularly after the medication is discontinued to ensure that your pressure remains normal—especially if you skip yoga at times. It is not necessary to get your blood pressure checked by a physician; you can do it yourself.

It is important to follow all the recommended practices in this book for high blood pressure, as each one contributes to normalise the pressure. Practising them correctly and in a relaxed way is also necessary. Though they are all extremely simple, I once had a nightmarish experience teaching them to an educated, successful businessman. When I asked him to concentrate on his breath, he would stop breathing. When I asked him to concentrate on his heartbeat, he tensed his muscles; and when I asked him to visualise a healthy heart, he said the thought of his heart made him feel nervous. It took all my skills to innovate practices he could relate to and eventually lower his blood pressure.

Successful treatment for high blood pressure partly depends on the patient's age and physical condition. An old person with degenerated blood vessels may find it difficult to make the blood pressure normal without medications. But yoga helps at any age and any stage.

CHAPTER TWO

High Blood Pressure and its Cure

The heart sends blood through blood vessels which, if joined lengthwise, would cover 75,000 miles. For blood to cruise through such long distances and in all possible directions, a pressure is required, which is created by the heart's contraction. This pressure is known as Blood Pressure. The pressure with which the blood leaves the heart is called the systolic, which is much higher than the pressure with which blood enters the heart on return and is known as diastolic. The systolic indicates how much force the heart is exerting to send the blood out into the blood vessels, while the diastolic shows how much the heart is relaxing. The ideal systolic pressure of a healthy adult is 120 and the diastolic should be 80, which is written as

15

120/80. Children's blood pressure is much lower than that such as 90/75. And in babies it is still lower. In old people it normally depends on their age. While generally their diastolic remains the same, their systolic may increase due to the natural degeneration of the arteries. The systolic pressure of such people is considered normal if the reading is their age plus a hundred. When the blood pressure measures higher then these accepted counts, it is called high blood pressure. A reading of 160/95 – 105 is considered as mild high blood pressure while 160 – 180/ 105 – 115 is regarded as moderately high. When it is over 180/ 115, it is labeled as severe high blood pressure.

Barring a few who experience some typical symptoms of high blood pressure, which are dizziness, breathlessness, palpitations, headaches, depression, sleeplessness, chest pain, loss of appetite, decreased memory and concentration and a flushed complexion, high blood pressure is generally a symptomless ailment.

Often patients come to know of their problem during a routine check-up or after some complications of the disease manifests. Unfortunately many times the first sign of high blood pressure is a fatal heart attack.

That is why high blood pressure has come to be known as a silent killer.

But with the following yogic routine, blood pressure can be normalised in a week's time.

Day 1

PAWANAMUKTASANA SERIES
Exercise 1

- Sit down with legs stretched out in front and hands on the floor behind the body. Close eyes and concentrate on your breath for a minute or two. Keep track of the natural rhythm of breathing. Count 5 breaths backwards.
- Open eyes.
- Inhale.
- Keeping the feet straight up, bend the toes forward while exhaling.
- Inhaling, bend them backwards.
- Repeat 10 times.

(It is important to synchronise with the natural breathing pattern i.e. when you pause a little after exhaling, there should be no movement at all.)

Yoga for a Healthy Heart

EXERCISE 2

- Exhaling, bend feet forward. Inhaling, bend them backwards. Repeat 10 times.
- Relax, close eyes and count 5 breaths backwards.

EXERCISE 3

- Move legs apart.
- Exhaling, rotate feet forwards and, inhaling, rotate them backwards.
- Repeat 10 times.
- Repeat in the other direction.
- Close eyes and count 5 breaths backwards.

Yoga for a Healthy Heart

EXERCISE 4

- Bring the legs close together. Place the right foot on the left thigh and place the right hand on the right knee. Holding the right foot with the left hand, rotate it 10 times in one direction, then 10 times in the other direction.
- Repeat for the other side.
- Close eyes and count 5 breaths backwards.

EXERCISE 5

- Grasp the left thigh with both hands. Inhaling, bend the leg pulling the knee to the chest, toes pointing upward. Exhaling, straighten the leg with the toes stretched out.
- Repeat 10 times.

- Similar exercise should be repeated with the right leg.
- Close eyes and count 10 breaths backwards.

EXERCISE 6

- Place legs wide apart, arms stretched out.
- Take a deep breath. Exhaling, turn your body to the left and touch the left foot with the right hand while the left arm remains in the same position.
- Inhaling, return to the starting position.
- Similar exercise should be done on the right side.
- Repeat 10 times.
- The movement should be continuous and in tune with your breathing.
- Close eyes and count 15 breaths backwards.

People with back ailments should avoid this exercise.

EXERCISE 7

- Keep the right foot on the left thigh. Place hands on the respective knees.
- Exhaling, press the right knee down to the floor.
- Inhaling, bring it up.
- Repeat 10 times.
- Similar exercise should be repeated with the left knee.
- Close eyes and count 5 breaths backwards.

EXERCISE 8

- Keep the right foot on the left thigh as close to the body as possible and hold the foot with your left hand.
- Hold the right knee with your right hand. Exhaling, rotate the knee downward.
- Inhaling, rotate it upward.
- Repeat 10 times in one direction and 10 times in the opposite direction.
- Straighten the legs and relax them.
- Similar exercise should be done with the left knee.
- Count 10 breaths backwards.

Yoga for a Healthy Heart

EXERCISE 9

- Fold the legs and join the feet facing each other.
- Holding the feet close to your body, move legs up and down fast. Breathing should be normal.
- Repeat it 10 times.
- Straighten the legs and relax.
- Close eyes and count 15 breaths backwards.
- Cross your legs and sit in *Sukhasana*.
- *Vajrasana* also can be assumed if *Sukhasana* is uncomfortable.

EXERCISE 10

- Extend arms in front.
- Bend the hands up from the wrists.
- Spread out the fingers.
- Clench and flex them 10 times breathing naturally.
- Bring the hands down to your lap and relax.
- Closing the eyes count 7 breaths backwards.

EXERCISE 11

- Extend arms in front.
- Keep the fingers together and palms facing down.
- Exhaling, bend hands downward.
- Inhaling, straighten them.
- Repeat 10 times.
- Placing the hands in your lap, close the eyes and count 7 breaths backwards.

EXERCISE 12

- Extend the arms as before. Close the hands into fists with the thumbs inside.
- Inhaling, rotate the wrists outward and exhaling rotate them inward.
- Repeat 10 times in one direction and 10 times in the opposite direction.
- Bring the hands, back to the lap, close eyes and count 7 breaths backwards.

EXERCISE 13

- Extend the arms again, palms facing up.
- Take a deep breath.
- Exhaling, bend the arms and touch the shoulders.
- Inhaling, straighten them.
- Repeat 10 times.
- Close eyes and count 7 breaths backwards.

Exercise 14

- Touch shoulders with the fingers of the respective hands.
- Inhaling, rotate arms backwards, exhaling rotate them forwards.
- Repeat 10 times in one direction and 10 times in the opposite direction.
- Relax, close eyes and count 10 breaths backwards.

Exercise 15

- Bend the head towards left shoulder and then towards right shoulder.
- Repeat 10 times.

EXERCISE 16

- Bend head forwards and backwards 10 times.

EXERCISE 17

- Rotate the head slowly 5 times in one direction and 5 times in the opposite direction.

The last two exercises should not be practised by people with cervical spondilitis.

- Lie down in *Shavasana*.
- Count 50 breaths backwards.

NADISODHAN PRANAYAMA

Rules

- For *Pranayama*, men should sit in *Siddhasana*.
- Women should sit in *Siddha Yoni Asana*.
- If the above is not possible, then sit in *Sukhasana* (the crossed leg posture).

Technique

- Sit straight.
- Keep the left hand on the left knee in *Gyan Mudra* or *Hriday Mudra* (page 52).
- Place the index and middle finger of the right hand on the forehead in between the eyebrows.
- Close the right nostril with the thumb.
- Take a deep breath in the natural speed from the left nostril. Closing the left nostril with the ring finger exhale from the right.
- In the same manner, inhale from the right and exhale from the left.
- Repeat the entire process 10 times.

Exhalations should take double the time of inhalations. For example — if you count 7 during inhalation you must count 14 during exhalation.

29

The numbers can be more or less depending on the capacity of your lungs. You must not feel uncomfortable at any stage. But the ratio of 1:2 must be maintained.

BHRAMARI PRANAYAMA

- Separate your teeth and close your mouth over it.
- Plug ears with your index fingers.
- Close your eyes and take a deep breath. As you exhale, make a humming sound stretching the breath till you are comfortable.
- Repeat 9 times.

End the session with meditation (page 89) and *Yoga Nidra* (page 95) daily till your blood pressure is normal and you have given up the medicines.

Day 2

After finishing *Pawanamuktasana* series (page 17) and before *Nadisodhan Pranayama*, practise the following *asanas*.

ANANDA MADIRASANA

Sit in *Vajrasana*.

Hold your ankles.

Cross your eyes and look at the point in between your eyebrows. Breathe slow and deep 20 times. Bring your hands to your lap and close your eyes.

SHASHANKASANA

- Sit in *Vajrasana*.
- Inhaling, raise arms.
- Exhaling bend forward.
  (The arm should remain straight and near the ears).
- Place forehead and forearms on the ground.
- Breathe normally 10 times. (Everyday add a few more breaths till you reach one hundred breaths).
- Finish with *Shavasana*, count 10 breaths backwards.

Day 3

After *Bhramari Pranayama* as per the previous day, practise *Sheetkari Pranayama*.

Technique

- Fold back your tongue. Join the teeth.
- Curl lips back.
- Breathe in slow and deep through the mouth producing a hissing sound.
- At the end of the inhalation, close mouth and exhale naturally from the nose. Repeat 9 times.

Day 4

- Practise 18 rounds of *Bhramari Pranayama* instead of 9.
- Add *Sheetli Pranayama* after *sheetkari pranayama*.

Technique of *Sheetli Pranayama:*

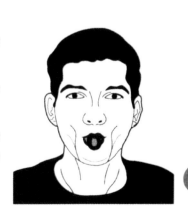

- Fold tongue lengthwise to resemble a tube and stick it out.
- Breathe in slow and deep through the tongue.
- Drawing the tongue back and closing the mouth, exhale from the nose. Practice 9 rounds.

Yoga for a Healthy Heart

Day 5

Same as the previous day, but increase *Sheetkari Pranayama* by 9 more rounds.

Day 6

Aasanas and *Pranayamas* are as before. In meditation, repeat the *Mantra Soham* in *Ujjayi Pranayama*.

Technique of *Ujjayi pranayama:*

Contract your throat a little, so that you can feel the breath there. When done correctly, your breaths will produce a mild hissing sound.

From the seventh day onward if the blood pressure is still high, practise *Ujjayi Pranayama*, whenever you can for as long as possible till your blood pressure has become normal.

Day 7

Bhramaripranayama, *Sheetli Pranayama* and *Sheetkari Pranayama* should be practised 27 times each. Continue this day's routine for another week.

CHAPTER THREE

Drug Danger

Because high blood pressure does not involve pain and is generally controlled by drugs, hypertensive people prefer to pop the pill and forget about their ailment rather than spend one hour on yoga. They do not seem to realise how these drugs are harming their system. These medicines are known to have the following effects.

■ DIURETICS

These medications cause the body to produce more urine and excrete sodium, leading to a drop in blood pressure. Side effects of these drugs may include hypotension (low blood pressure), fatigue, muscle weakness, loss of appetite,

37

constipation, and potassium depletion–which in turn can lead to cardiac arrhythmia. Diuretics may have an adverse effect on sugar metabolism and raise the blood sugar level. The uric acid level may also go up, leading to gout and arthritis. One type of diuretic is even known to increase blood cholesterol. Sometimes it causes hypotonia due to potassium loss.

▓ BETA-BLOCKERS
These drugs suppress the sympathetic nervous system — whose job is to gear-up the body parts to work — thereby decreasing the heart rate. At the same time these lessen the force with which the heart muscle contract and reduce blood vessel contraction in the heart, brain, and throughout the body. While the slow pulse rate effectively reduces blood pressure, it also reduces circulation to peripheral parts of the body which can result in malnourishment of the peripheral body tissues and cause unusual tiredness, sensitivity to cold and sunlight and hurt exercise tolerance. Beta-blockers also aggravate asthma.

▓ METHYLDOPA
This drug is related to dopamine and hence can cause drowsiness and depression. It can also damage the liver.

▓ PERIPHERAL VASODILATORS
These drugs dilate blood capillaries and can lead to hypotension and fainting.

38

■ CLORIDINE

It inhibits the hypothalamic and other brain centers blocking the transmission of impulses from the brain to the blood vessels with the result that arterial resistance and blood pressure drop. Side effects can lead to impaired mental functioning and nervous system disorder.

Though the drugs are harmful, it may be necessary to take them initially as leaving the ailment uncontrolled can be dangerous. Once a gentleman had come to me to treat his high blood pressure. To motivate him to continue with his practice regularly, I had told him that the ill effects of the anti-hypertensive drugs were worse than the ailment itself. Years later, he brought his young son who had very high blood pressure and proudly announced that he did not allow his son to take the medication! Fortunately the boy's ailment was at an early stage and did not do any harm.

As high blood pressure decreases blood flows to body tissues, but if left untreated it can lead to serious and irreversible conditions such as:

Brain damage

Serious problems that can develop due to weakening of brain tissues are encephalopathy and Alzheimer's disease. According to a study in Finland, people with hypertension and high level of cholesterol have nearly eight times the risk of getting Alzheimer's disease than those with normal levels. At a milder level, high blood pressure can lead to loss of memory and concentration.

Kidney damage

The kidneys are important organs, which are supplied with one fifth of the total volume of blood pumped by the heart. When these vital organs do not receive the usual amount they react violently by releasing an enzyme called rennin, which causes the blood vessels to contract to force the heart to pump harder. The blood pressure rises leading to further decrease in the blood supply to the kidneys, which in turn results in more rennin secretion. A vicious cycle is thus formed leading to the gradual failure of these vital organs. When the kidneys do not function well the balance of salts, acids and water goes haywire and toxins pile up, which invariably causes death.

Eye problem

With less blood supply, the delicate optic nerves and muscles start degenerating, leading to blurring, double vision and gradual or sudden loss of eyesight.

Blood vessel damage

The constant high pressure against the walls of the blood vessels causes them to stiffen. As a protective reaction, these vessels start thickening resulting in arteriosclerosis, a condition where the blood vessels are rigid and brittle and are prone to rupture.

40

Atherosclerosis

Small scars appear in the inner walls of blood vessels. These wounds are covered with plaque making the arteries thicker and stiffer, resulting in more wounds. Gradually the passage becomes narrow and these narrowed arteries not only restrict blood flow to important body parts but a plaque can get dislodged and block the passage cutting off the blood supply completely resulting in heart attack.

Stroke

A stiffened artery can rupture in the brain causing a stroke. A blood clot or a piece of plaque can also cause a stroke by blocking an artery supplying blood to the brain.

Heart damage

The inflexible arteries exert a tremendous pressure on the heart. To keep up with the ever-increasing load, the heart increases in size, which may make its muscle stiff. This decreases the efficiency of the heart. Blood is not circulated well enough, causing fluid accumulation in various parts of the body including the lungs. To clear the congestion, the heart struggles harder, which may result in a heart failure due to sheer exhaustion.

41

All these damages can be prevented if yoga is taken up early enough.

After stabilising the pressure over a period of few months, the following yogic cleansing technique should be practiced to remove the harmful chemicals of the anti-hypertention drugs from the body.

It is practiced first thing in the morning on empty stomach. Start by drinking six glasses of luke warm water, and then practice the following a*sanas*.

PADASANCHALANASANA (CYCLING)

- Lie down on your back.
- Lift the legs up.
- Move your legs forward as in a cycling motion.
- Do it ten times.
- Then move them backwards ten times.

Yoga for a Healthy Heart

Suptaudarakarshanasana (side rolling)

Lie down on your back. Interlock your fingers and keep your hands under the head.

Bend the legs and bring the knees over to the chest.

Keeping the knees and feet together, lower the knees to the floor on the left side while turning your head to the right side.

Quickly repeat the movement on the right side.

Practice this twenty times without pausing.

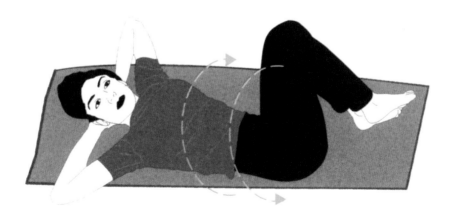

KAWACHALASANA

- Squat on the floor.
- Keep your hands on your knees.
- Move your body forward, placing your right knee on the ground.
- Take the left foot forward and place the left knee on the ground.
- Walk on the floor in this manner.
- Take as many steps as you can without feeling strained.
- Visit the toilet as often as you want and empty your bowels.
- Practice this as often as you can.

(All *asanas* mentioned in this chapter are meant for people with normal blood pressure and a healthy heart.)

CHAPTER FOUR

Heart Attack

eart attack is a major killer in the world, which occurs mostly due to stress and unhealthy coronary arteries. When these arteries are healthy, they are elastic with a smooth inner wall, without any scars or plaque. They expand easily to receive the surge of blood coming from the right ventricle. Whenever the heart muscle requires extra blood for some extra work, they expand still more and carry the excess volume. But if the demand for blood continues to remain high over long periods, these arteries remain overstretched constantly, which in the long run makes them lose their elasticity. Various factors, especially physical and mental stress also scar and wound the arterial wall. As we have already discussed, the body

47

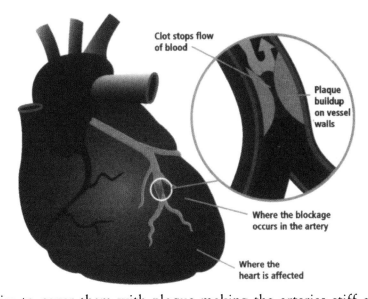

Clot stops flow of blood

Plaque buildup on vessel walls

Where the blockage occurs in the artery

Where the heart is affected

tries to cover them with plaque making the arteries stiff and liable to more wounds leading to more plaque covering. The arteries thus become stiffer and narrower. These worn and rigid arteries can no longer expand to meet any excess demand of the heart muscle. As a result, the muscle that is deprived of the required amount of oxygen can cramp, bringing about pain and discomfort. In a milder form this condition is known as angina pectoris. Angina pain generally lasts for a few minutes and is relieved by rest and relaxation, as that decreases the oxygen requirement. In its severe form, the pain persists in spite of rest and is termed as heart attack, a condition, where the blood supply to the heart muscle is completely cut off. Generally, a blood clot from the arterial wall gets dislodged and blocks an artery feeding the heart tissues. The starved tissues die rapidly and are never replaced. If the affected area is small and the heart's electrical system is not damaged, the victim may survive. Otherwise a heart attack can spell sure death.

A heart attack may happen all of a sudden or may give indication in the form of pain and discomfort, hours, days or even weeks before the actual attack. The main symptom of a heart attack is intense and prolonged chest pain. Victims describe it to be like a powerful squeezing sensation. The pain often radiates to the left shoulder, left arm or both arms, back, neck and jaw. Sometimes, pain is felt in the upper abdomen also, which is like severe indigestion pain. Other symptoms of a heart attack can be profuse perspiration, irregular heartbeat, nervousness, and shortness of breath, vomiting, fainting and overwhelming weakness.

Heart attack can also occur without any pain. A research showed that more than thirty percent of heart attack victims that came to a hospital, had felt no chest pain whatsoever. The lack of pain makes patients seek medical help later than necessary, which can have a fatal consequence. In fact these patients are twice as likely to succumb to the attack. What adds to the woe is that sometimes doctors too may not diagnose and react quickly enough to save the patient. Most old people above the age of 75 are more likely to have painless heart attack as do women and people with diabetes, stroke or earlier heart failure.

Heart attack is a medical emergency. Survival depends on the speed at which treatment is started. Often death occurs in the first fifteen minutes before medical help can be reached. Even with proper treatment, the first two hours are risky. If one

49

survives this period, it is almost certain that the person will live. After twenty-four hours, the risk of death becomes almost nil.

Sometimes, people mistake the discomfort of heart attack as gas pain and ignore it. This can have serious consequences. I personally knew a gentleman who found himself in a similar situation. His mild abdominal pain, which he thought was due to flatulence, did not abate even after taking antacid. As it was midnight he hesitated to wake up his family members or even call a doctor. Finally when the doctor arrived in the morning his condition was beyond repair. A major part of his heart muscle was dead. And even with the best medical treatment he did not survive. Therefore no time should be wasted if one experiences any of the symptoms of a heart attack in seeking medical help.

Till medical help arrives one should try not to exert at all. To minimise the energy usage of the body *Shavasana* is very effective. To enhance relaxation, *Yoga Nidra* should be practiced. If possible *Coronary Pranayama* and *Hriday Mudra* should be practiced in *Shavasan*. Sometimes heart attack is the result of stress related spasm. With the above techniques such an attack can even be averted.

After the heart attack has been treated in the hospital, to speed up the recovery a patient needs to be calm and well relaxed. But usually at this stage the patient is tense and fearful, thinking of his predicament ceaselessly. *Yoga Nidra,* soft music and various chants successfully divert the patient's mind and induce deep relaxation. Later, when the condition improves, the following yogic techniques can be introduced with the consent

50

of the treating physician. These practices need no effort at all and are highly beneficial for the heart.

SHAVASANA

During this *asana* the oxygen requirement of the body is minimal which provides the best possible rest to the heart.

Technique:

- Lie down and your back with feet about eighteen inches apart. Place hands by your side and a little away from the body, palms facing up. The eyes should be gently shut. Relax and count your breaths backwards from 100.

UTTHANA PADASANA

- Lie down on your back with the feet on a thick pillow. This *asana* facilitates better blood flow to the heart muscles. One can also place a pillow under the head.

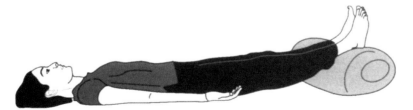

HRIDAY MUDRA

- This is a hand gesture that sends a strong current of energy or life force to the heart and strengthens it.
- Touch the base of the thumb with the tip of the index finger of the same hand.
- Join the tips of thumbs, middle and ring fingers. The little finger should remain straight and away from the joined fingers.
- Concentrate on the rise and fall of the chest.
- Alternatively, concentrate on your natural breathing.
- Practice it for 20 to 30 minutes.

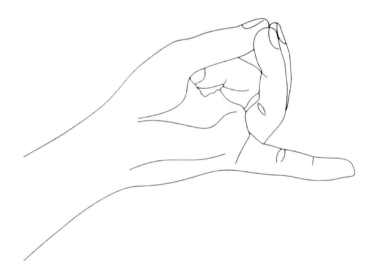

Anulom Viloma

This is a simple meditative practice which can be done anywhere, any time and in any position.

Concentrate on your breaths. Breathing should be absolutely spontaneous. After a few minutes, imagine you are breathing in from the left nostril and breathing out from the right then breathing in from the right nostril and breathing out from the left. After a while make the exhalation slower and longer. It should be double the duration of inhalation. Practice it for as long as you can.

With time, rest, and these yogic practices the heart will recover to do its normal daily work. When the treating doctor gives the go ahead sign for mild exercises, start yoga without delay. The practices recommended for high blood pressure are mild enough for heart patients and are extremely effective.

Coronary Pranayam

Practice *Anulom Viloma* in *Ujjayi* with the mantra *Soham* or any other mantra in 1:2 ratio, that is if 3 mantras are repeated during inhalation, exhalation should be of six mantras.

53

Risk Factors
and
Yogic Remedies

CHAPTER FIVE

Risk Factors and Yogic Remedies

Some people are more prone to have heart diseases than others and should take the necessary precautions if they have any of the following risk factors.

▇ HEREDITY

It has been seen that, children whose both parents have high blood pressure have 45% more chances to get the ailment than children of parents with normal blood pressure. If one of the parents has hypertension, the chances of inheriting the disease are reduced by 15%.

▇ SMOKING

This harmful addiction tops the list of avoidable risk factors.

Statistics have revealed that smoking increases sudden cardiac death by 100%. Tobacco harms the cardiovascular system in more ways than one.

a) It stimulates the adrenal glands to secrete a hormone, whose presence in the blood constricts the blood vessels, resulting in higher blood pressure and faster heart beat.

b) It increases platelets clumping which is the chief cause for cholesterol deposit on the arterial wall. Such deposit, further, narrows the blood vessels thereby raising the blood pressure. It accelerates the process of arteriosclerosis.

c) Smoking also hardens the blood vessels leading to greater peripheral resistance.

d) The carbon monoxide of tobacco is seen to bind with the red blood cells taking the place of valuable oxygen. The decreased oxygen in the blood leads to the deterioration of all body tissues including that of the heart and the blood vessels.

e) Carbon monoxide itself is responsible for the degeneration of the entire cardiovascular system. Cigarette smoke is such a potent poison that even in a passive smoker it causes untold damage. Smokers with high blood pressure run ten times greater risk than smokers with normal blood pressure.

■ HIGH FAT DIET

Next to smoking a high fat diet is the big risk factor. If the body receives more fat than its need, the fat in the blood increases, making the blood thicker. To pump thicker blood, the heart has to work harder resulting in higher blood pressure.

■ OVERWEIGHT

Obese people are more prone to high blood pressure and heart attacks than normal people, because the heart gets strained working overtime to provide blood to all those extra tissues. It has been seen that every pound of excess fat contains 200 miles of blood capillaries. Also, obese people have been found to have lower HDL cholesterol, which increased when they lost weight. This cholesterol has a beneficial effect on the blood vessels.

■ SEDENTARY LIFE

Like other muscles of the body, the heart too needs exercise to remain toned and healthy. Lack of exercise can make it and the blood vessels weak and inefficient. A weak muscle can no longer circulate the blood effectively throughout the body while the weak blood vessels offer greater resistance making the blood pressure go up.

People who belong to the above mentioned groups should not be complacent and ignore the danger they are facing, but do the needful and prevent all heart ailments. First, the smokers need to quit smoking at the earliest. Resolution during *Yoga Nidra* or yogic sleep (page 95) is the most effective way to achieve

57

that. A suggestion made by another person to that effect while the person is sleeping lightly is also quite effective. My brother was a chain smoker in his younger days and had no intention of giving it up. My worried mother asked me what should be done. An idea came to me and I thought of trying it out on him. I suggested that she should go to his bedroom every day early in the morning while he was still sleeping and to whisper in his ears 'Give up smoking' and repeat the sentence thrice. My bachelor brother never locked his door those days, which made it easier for my mother to do this daily. Within a month he quit smoking saying he did not enjoy it anymore! Much later when we told him how it was done, he was aghast and never left his door unlocked thereafter!

A sensible low calorie diet with fifty rounds of *Suryanamaskar* (starting with five rounds, the number should be gradually increased over a period of a few months) is excellent to counter the above risk factors.

SURYANAMASKAR

Note: People with a weak back or high blood pressure should not attempt this practice.

- Stand with feet joined and hands folded in front of the chest.

- Inhaling raise hands and bend backwards.
- Exhaling bend forward and place the hands flat on the floor. You may bend the knees in the beginning.
- Inhaling stretch the right leg back while bending the left knee and lowering the torso. Stretch the neck backwards.

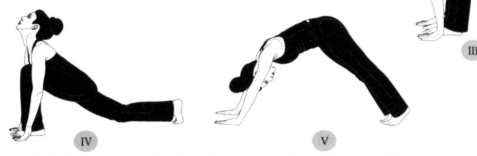

Exhaling, take the left foot back to join the right one while lifting the hips to form a triangle with your body.

- Holding your breath, lower the body to the ground, keeping the pelvis up.
- Drop the pelvis, and inhaling, lift up your body from the navel, looking upward and straighten the arms.
- Exhaling assume the position of Step 5.
- Inhaling bring the left foot forward to assume posture 4.
- Exhaling assume posture 3.
- Inhaling assume posture 2.
- Exhaling return to the starting position.

Yoga for a Healthy Heart

Practice as above with the right foot in front to complete one round. Lie down in *Shavasana* till breathing becomes normal.

■ DIABETES

Diabetes is a major risk factor for heart ailments. Every second diabetic sooner or later suffers from blood vessel damage increasing the blood pressure and running the increased risk of a heart attack. Women are the worse victims, they are five times more prone to coronary heart disease than people with normal blood sugar, while male diabetics have double the risk.

Diabetes can be completely cured with Yoga but the treatment must be undertaken under strict supervision. People with a family history of this ailment should strengthen their pancreas through the following *asanas* to prevent diabetes.

ARDHAMATSYENDRASANA

- Sit on the floor, with legs stretched in front.
- Folding the right leg, place the foot on the left side, the heel touching the left hip.
- Bend the left leg upright, placing the foot in front of the right knee.
- Taking the right hand over the left leg, hold the left ankle.
- Take the left hand behind and place the back of the hand on the right side of the waist.
- Look straight ahead and take a deep breath.
- Maintaining a straight posture, exhale and twist from the waist to the left, to look back over the shoulder.
- Take ten normal breaths (to be increased to twenty over a few days).

Inhale, return to the starting position.

Repeat on the other side.

GOMUKHASANA

Sit and fold the legs, to keep the right knee over the left one and heels touching the opposite sides of the hips.

Take the left hand back.

Lifting the right arm up, hold hands at the behind.

Maintain a straight posture, with the right elbow pointing straight up.

Take ten normal breaths (to be increased to twenty over a few days).

Repeat on the other side.

Yoga for a Healthy Heart

YOGAMUDRASANA

Sit in the *Vajrasana*.

Close hands into fists and place them on the respective thighs, close to the trunk.

Exhaling, bend forward and place the forehead on the floor.

Take five normal breaths (to be increased to twenty or thirty).

Inhaling, sit up.

Lie down in *Shavasana*.

Uddiyana Bandha

- Sit in *Padmasana* (lotus pose).

- Place hands on the knees.

- Breathing out through puckered lips, bend your head forward to rest the chin against the chest.

- Pull in your stomach.

- Hold the posture till comfortable.

- Release the stomach.

- Lift your head and inhale, take a few breaths before repeating it again.

- Repeat five times.

▊ AGE

Though stress in modern times is leading to high blood pressure in young people, it is the middle-aged men and women who are generally affected by cardiovascular ailments. Yoga practitioners maintain healthy cardiovascular system even in old age.

■ GENDER

Generally men are more prone to heart attacks than women. The male hormone testosterone is vastly responsible for it. If this hormone is in excess in the blood, its molecules get affixed to cardiac receptors, wounding and weakening the heart muscle gradually. *Siddhasana* controls the testosterone secretion preventing damage to the heart.

SIDDHASANA

- Sit with legs stretched in front.
- Bend the left leg and sit on the left foot, the heel pressing against the perineum.
- Fold the right leg on the left one, the heel against the body and the ankle on top of the left ankle.
- Push the right toe in-between the calf and the thigh of the left leg.
- Bring the left toe in-between the thigh and the calf of the right leg.
- Keep the hands on the knees in *Gyan Mudra*.
- Sit straight and breathe normally, for five to ten minutes.
- Practice twice daily.

(All *asanas* mentioned in this chapter are meant for people with normal blood pressure and a healthy heart.)

CHAPTER SIX

Yogic Cardiovascular System

E ven in the absence of any of the risk factors mentioned in the previous chapter, some people still suffer a heart attack. Therefore, it is wiser to do the needful to maintain the best possible health of the cardiovascular system.

The cardiovascular system, with the heart at its apex, is one of the most important systems in the human body. Understanding the structure and function of this system will help us do beneficial things and avoid potential threats.

The cardiovascular system consists of the heart, blood vessels, and blood. The heart is a hollow organ made up of strong muscles. It is separated into two sections—the left and the right—by a muscular wall. Each part has two chambers, one on top of the other. Each chamber has a gate called a valve that opens in only one direction to prevent blood from returning after it leaves a chamber. The upper chambers are the left atrium and the right atrium; the lower chambers are the left and right ventricles.

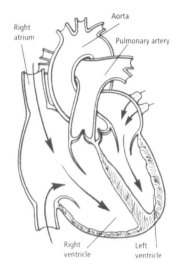

The right atrium receives used blood collected from all over the body, and then passes it on to the ventricle below. From there, the blood is sent to the lungs where it gives up waste and takes oxygen from inhaled air. Then it moves to the left atrium. From here, blood flows into the left ventricle, which then contracts to push the blood out to all the parts of the body, where it will deliver food, water and oxygen to the tissues and collect their waste matter.

Thus, the heart goes on pumping sixty-two to seventy-five times a minute (much faster for many people). It will beat roughly two and a half billion times in a single lifetime without ever stopping. For such a small organ to perform such a mammoth task, the heart needs extra strong, resilient muscles.

The following *asanas* will exercise the

heart and make it stronger. The stretching movements mentioned here stretch and flex the blood vessels, keeping them healthy and elastic.

Akarna Dhanurasana

- Stand straight with feet apart along the lines of the shoulders.
- Take the right foot forward.
- Lift the right arm in front with hand closed into a fist to the eye level. The arm should be along the same line as the right leg.
- Close the left hand into a fist and keep it near the right one.
- Turn head slightly to the right to look at the right hand.

Yoga for a Healthy Heart

- Inhaling, pull the left hand back to the left ear while tilting backwards.
- Hold the posture for a comfortable duration.
- Exhaling, come forward and repeat it.
- Practice five times.
- Change position and repeat five times on the other side.

Hastauthanasana

- Stand with legs wide apart.
- Cross hands at the wrists in front.
- Inhaling, lift arms above the head.
- Holding the breath spread the arms out, down and then up again.
- Exhaling, bring them down.
- Repeat ten times.

71

Ardhachandrasana

- Kneel down.
- Take out the left foot to place it flat on the ground and take a step forward.
- Place the hands on both sides of the foot.
- Take the right foot back and stretch the leg well.
- Inhaling, lift arms above you, bend backwards and stretch the chest.
- Exhaling, return to the starting position.
- Repeat on the other side.

Proper oxygenation of the blood is essential for cardiac health. For this, our body needs lungs that expand and contract well. Also, people generally don't breathe deeply, letting stale air settle at the bottom of the lungs where most of the blood vessels lie. This restricts the exchange of gases. A yogic *Pranayama* called *Kapalabhati* expels stale air from the lungs, making room for fresh air and improving the health of the lungs by drawing more blood into their vessels.

KAPALBHATI PRANAYAMA

- Assume the posture for *Nadisodhan Pranayama*.
- Breathe in naturally and exhale with a force 20 times, first through the left nostril, then the right and then through both. This is one round. Gradually increase to 5 rounds.

73

To make the lungs healthier, *Sarvangasana* and *Matsyasana* are excellent.

SARVANGASANA

- Lie down on your back.
- Holding your trunk, push your body up to assume a perpendicular posture.
- Breathe normally for a minute. (20 breaths)
- Bend your legs and slowly bring your body down. Try not to lift the head in the process.

MATSYASANA

- Sit in *Padmasana, Ardhapadmasana* or simply stretch your legs in front of you.
- Bending your head backwards, push your chest out.
- Maintain your body arch with the help of your arms, lower the head backwards towards the ground (the corner of the head should take the weight).
- Hold your big toes if you can or just place your hands on your thighs.

74

- Breathe deeply for half a minute i.e half the duration of *Sarvangasana*.
- Return to the starting position.
- Lie down in *Shavasana* for ten breaths.

People practicing this *asana* in *Ardhapadmasana* should practice on the other side as well.

Yoga for a Healthy Heart

Blood travels in two types of blood vessels: arteries and veins. Arteries carry oxygenated blood from the heart to the tissues, while veins carry used blood from the body to the heart. The

Blood Circulation
Principal Veins and Arteries

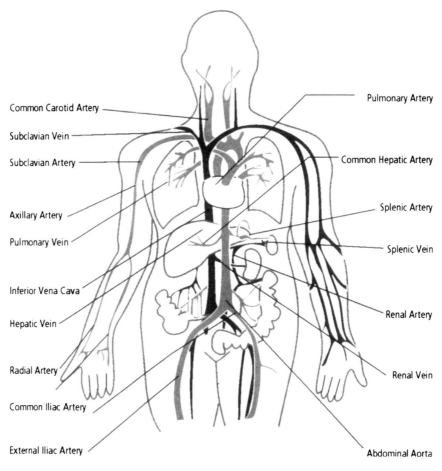

Common Carotid Artery

Subclavian Vein

Subclavian Artery

Axillary Artery

Pulmonary Vein

Inferior Vena Cava

Hepatic Vein

Radial Artery

Common Iliac Artery

External Iliac Artery

Pulmonary Artery

Common Hepatic Artery

Splenic Artery

Splenic Vein

Renal Artery

Renal Vein

Abdominal Aorta

Yoga for a Healthy Heart

arteries are mostly elastic. As blood leaves the heart in surges, the elasticity of the arteries makes it possible for them to expand, breaking the surge into a smooth flow.

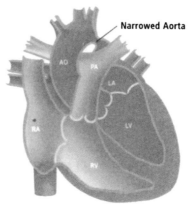

Coarctation of the Aorta

Narrowed Aorta

AO = Aorta
PA = Pulmonary Artery
LA = Left Atrium
RA = Right Atrium
LV = Left Ventricle
RV = Right Ventricle

The aorta, the body's largest artery, lies closest to the heart and receives blood first. It branches into smaller and smaller arteries and turns muscular. The thinnest blood vessels, known as capillaries, are so narrow that in normal circumstances red blood cells must squeeze through them in single file, often twisting themselves into odd shapes as they pass.

The blood's return journey begins after it collects debris from the tissues. The tiny capillaries unite to form venules, which join to make larger and larger veins that ultimately terminate at the heart.

The heart muscles need blood for themselves. Though the organ is filled with blood, it cannot draw oxygenated blood for its own use. Two special blood vessels called coronary arteries provide blood to the heart tissues. When the heart needs more blood for extra work, these arteries provide it by dilating.

Needless to say, all of our blood vessels should be elastic, relaxed, and free from deposits on their inner walls, to allow blood to freely pass through them. Any tension can constrict

77

these vessels, including the capillaries, and lead to inadequate nourishment for body tissues.

Yogic relaxation techniques especially, *Yoga Nidra,* effectively relax the blood vessels, while yogic *asanas* such as the *Pawanamuktasana* series, help maintain their elasticity even in old age. For healthy coronary arteries, *Shalabhasana,* is extremely beneficial.

Shalabhasana

In this *asana,* blood flows naturally to the heart and the coronary arteries and improves their health.

- Lie face down with your forehead on the ground.
- Keep the hands under the thighs, palms facing down.
- Take a deep breath.
- Lift the legs as high as you feel comfortable.

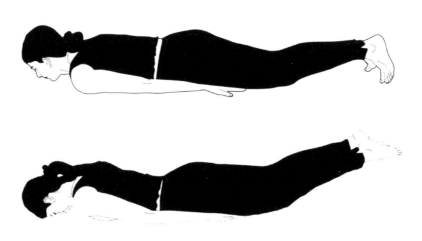

- Hold your breath and your posture for a few seconds.
- Exhaling, bring the legs down and relax.
- After a few breaths, repeat it again.
- Repeat five times.
- Gradually, increase the duration of the final posture for as long as you can.

The yogic techniques mentioned in this chapter are basic preventive measures to keep the cardiovascular system fit and are not meant for heart patients. People with essential hypertension can practice these *asanas* only after normalising their blood pressure and letting it stabilise for at least four months. Other yogic practices may be added according to your inclination and requirements.

More about Blood Pressure

H a disease. It is only a t the heart is labouring ressure never remains ιy people. It keeps fluctuating all the time. At night when we sleep, the energy requirement of the body tissues are the minimum, causing ninety percent of the capillaries to shut down, and the blood pressure falls to the lowest minimum. During the day, it rises as and when the energy requirement of the body increases. For example the energy our leg muscles need for climbing stairs or running is much more than what they need for strolling. Accordingly, the blood pressure during the former activity is higher than the latter. But when one

Blood pressure is elevated

is standing erect, blood flows downward which reduces the heart's work and the blood pressure shows that by falling low. The blood pressure in the morning is generally lower than in the evening. It also varies from season to season. In colder months it is higher than in warmer months. Emotions such as anger, fright and excitement can push the blood pressure up instantaneously. Visiting a doctor for a routine checkup is enough to raise the blood pressure of many people. That is why a wise doctor takes 2 - 3 readings in order to determine the actual blood pressure of a person. The first reading is usually higher than the second and the second higher than the third. Some medicines such as oral contraceptives can also raise the blood pressure.

In all the above-mentioned cases the elevation of blood pressure is temporary and as soon as the situation changes the blood pressure too drops to its normal reading. Only if the blood pressure remains constantly high over a period it is termed

Blood pressure Falls

Yoga for a Healthy Heart

as high blood pressure. High blood pressure is called essential hypertension when it is not complicated by a serious ailment such as diabetes or by a high level of blood lipid and cholesterol. Earlier, only old people in their fifties and sixties were affected by high blood pressure. Later, people in their thirties and forties started getting it, but now, youngsters are getting it too. What is disturbing is that a chunk of school children are also found to be hypertensive.

LOW BLOOD PRESSURE

When the heart exerts less pressure than usual and relaxes more than necessary, the blood pressure drops below the normal range, its a condition termed as hypotension or low blood pressure. A mild hypotension measuring 110/70 is generally preferred as it puts less strain on the internal organs but when it is lower than that, it can have unpleasant symptoms and sometimes even harm the system.

Low blood pressure, is caused by various factors such as anemia, severe blood loss, and pregnancy. The pressure becomes normal when the causative factors change. Often, people have low blood pressure with no apparent reasons and are subject to symptoms such as nausea, weakness, giddiness, sinking feeling in abdomen and even fainting. The symptoms are more prominent when the person rises suddenly from a sitting position. Generally, there is no medical treatment for fluctuating or low blood pressure but Yoga normalises the internal condition and stabilises the pressure.

The following routine is excellent to elevate the blood pressure of people who suffer from hypotension.

KATICHAKRASANA

- Stand with legs apart with arms stretched out on the sides at shoulder level.
- Swing the trunk to the left and keep the right hand on the left shoulder while the left hand goes back to rest on the right waist with your palms outward.
- Look back over your left shoulder.
- Quickly swing to practice on the other side.
- Repeat ten times.
- The movement should be continuous.

TRIKONASANA

- Stand straight with legs apart and arms stretched out sideways at shoulder level.

- Take a deep breath.

- Exhaling and maintaining the position of the arms, bend sideways to the right.

- Bending the right knee, touch the foot.

- Turn face up to look at the left hand.

- Inhaling, return to the standing position.

- Practice on the other side.

- Repeat ten times.

- If you feel giddy practicing any of the above *asanas*, discontinue. Instead, do the *Pawanamuktasana* series but without concentrating on the breaths and also without any rest in between the exercises.

- After a week or two, again try the major ones.

Vipareeta Karani Mudra

- Practice *Sarvangasana* and slightly lower your hips so that your trunk makes a 45% degree angle with the floor.
- Hold the posture for a minute.
- Slowly return to the starting position.
- After ten breaths rest, practice *Shashankasana*.

Bhastrika Pranayama

- Sit in *Padmasana* or *Sukhasana* with left hand on the knee in *Gyan Mudra*.
- Place the right hand on forehead like *Nadisodan Pranayama*.
- Close the right nostril. Forcefully and rapidly breathe from the left nostril twenty times.

Yoga for a Healthy Heart

- Do the same on the right side twenty times.
- This is one round. Practice one to three rounds in summer and three to five rounds in winter.

SURYABHEDA PRANAYAMA
- Sit like the previous *Pranayama*, closing the left nostril with the ring finger.
- Inhale deeply and slowly from the right nostril.
- Closing both nostrils and holding the breath, bend your head down so that the chin rests on the chest.
- Contract your perineum.
- Maintain your posture for few seconds.
- Relax your perineum.
- Lift your head.
- Closing your left nostril, exhale from the right.
- Practice five to ten rounds.

(All *asanas* mentioned in this chapter are meant for people with a healthy heart.)

CHAPTER EIGHT

Meditation

Emotions have a strong influence on one's heart. It keeps changing its behavior according to a persons moods and feelings. We all know how it thuds away when we are angry or excited. We also have heard that it can stop when one is very sad. Tragic news, sudden fright and even over excitement have caused many a death due to sudden cardiac arrest. No wonder tense and sad people are more prone to be affected by heart ailments. But to remain relaxed and cheerful when things go against you is not easy. Our daily routine can be subjected to much tension and anxiety. How can one relax when the person is constantly dealing with innumerable problems—deadlines, delays, diseases, deaths, disabled relatives, difficult boss,

89

accidents, unpleasant neighbours, violence, poverty, government rules, loneliness and natural calamities? We naturally get angry when we are abused and humiliated, and, anger is our worst enemy. It stimulates the adrenal glands to pump adrenalin into the blood stream, leading to shallow breathing, palpitation, and elevated blood pressure. Intense anger can also cause a sudden heart attack and even death.

Everybody does not experience the same emotions in the same degree in a similar situation. Our response to a situation depends on our own inner nature. Some get angry and irritated at the slightest provocation even though they know the corroding effect has this emotion on their system. But to gain control over one's emotions, a persons desire to do so is not enough. One needs to change one's inner nature which can happen automatically through meditation.

The word mediation aptly represents the calm countenance of a yogi, sitting still in the lotus pose, with eyes closed, unaware of his surrounding, unruffled by personal tragedies and unperturbed by human emotions.

Meditation is known to transform people for the better. The sage of the great Indian epic *Ramayana,* Valmiki started out as a cruel dacoit, Ratnakara, who robbed and killed people mercilessly for a living. The celestial sage, Narada, made him realise his sin and instructed him to repeat the mantra 'Ram'. The dacoit obeyed and with this mantra-meditation turned into a peaceful and enlightened sage. The story might be mythological but the message is not. My Guru or spiritual master,

Paramahansa Swami Sri Satyananda Saraswati, taught meditation to many hardened criminals and made them turn away completely from crime. In recent times, meditation has been taught to the inmates of the Tihar Jail of Delhi with wonderful results. They have become kind, tolerant and averse to violence.

Meditation affects not just the mind but also the body. The effect of meditation on the physical body is instantaneous. Experiments with scientific instruments reveal that during meditation the oxygen consumption of the body decreases drastically. In 10 minutes it drops by 20% and in half an hour it is less by 80% indicating the lack of activities of the body tissues or rather, it's restful state. When breathing is slow and deep, the heartbeat too becomes slow and steady and the brain emits alpha and theta waves—all signs of a highly relaxed body and mind. A meditator gradually becomes more and more relaxed and cheerful and his or her blood pressure remains stable. Although any meditation can be practiced with the same result, I generally teach the following one to my high blood pressure and heart patients.

Technique:

- Sit down in a meditative posture preferably *Siddhasana* for men and *Siddha Yoni Asana* for women with hands on the knees in *Gyan Mudra*.
- Close your eyes.
- Straighten your body.

91

- Sit still throughout the practice.
- If you are unable to sit for 20-25 minutes due to a weak back, practise meditation in *Shavasana*, but guard against dozing off during the practice.
- Relax the body.
- Visualise your body from tip to toe.
- Concentrate on your breaths.
- Feel them in your nose.
- Do not let your mind move away from your breaths. If it does, follow it for a while then gently bring it back.
- Continue for 4-5 minutes.
- Then follow your breaths down to your chest, nose to chest, then chest to nose.
- Practise for 2-3 minutes.
- Imagine you are inhaling fresh green air. After 2-3 minutes take your mind inside the chest.
- See the green air surround the heart and getting absorbed into it.
- After 2–3 minutes bring your attention back to your breaths.
- Now visualise a transparent tube between your throat and navel.
- Imagine you are breathing through the tube.
- When you inhale, your breath rises from the navel to the throat and when you exhale, it falls from the throat to the navel.

Yoga for a Healthy Heart

- After 2-3 minutes add the *mantra Sohum* to your breaths.
- Mentally repeat 'so' when you inhale and '*hum*' when you exhale.
- Continue it for around 10 minutes.
- Discontinue mantra repetition.
- Visualise a green candle flame in your heart or in the centre of your eyebrow and concentrate on it for 2-3 minutes. You can also concentrate on an object of your choice.
- At the end of the practice take your mind out to the surroundings.
- Take a deep breath.
- As you exhale chant *mmm*...
- Repeat 7 times.
- Open your eyes.

93

CHAPTER NINE

Yoga Nidra

After a day's hard work of supplying blood to various body parts, the heart needs a good night's sleep to rest and rejuvenate itself. Lack of sleep can spell serious trouble for this important organ. I know of a renowned cardiologist from a reputed hospital who suddenly had a heart attack. The news shocked all who knew him. He, a lean health conscious doctor with healthy habits and no vices, seemed the least likely candidate for such a problem. On enquiry I discovered that prior to the heart attack, this doctor had attended a series of functions at various places in close succession. Due to delayed and cancelled flights, he had to travel by road most of the time, and, at times throughout the night in order to

95

reach the various venues on time. Consequently he got almost no rest. Obviously his exhausted heart collapsed. This doctor was not a young man. But young people too should not take their hearts for granted. Recently I read a Reuter's report that said that a twenty eight year old South Korean man who played computer games non-stop for fifty hours died of heart failure minutes after finishing the mammoth session.

But modern life style does not afford the rest the heart so badly needs. It is called upon too frequently to supply extra blood for all our extra work, which includes excessive thinking, planning, calculating, talking, discussing and socialising. Late nights and heavy dinners add to the woe, because not only the heart's sleeping time cut short, also, it is burdened with additional work of supplying extra blood to the digestive system for hours during its resting period. The shortened sleep itself not too deep as several factors such as fear, anger, anxiety and worry prevent sound sleep. With increased work and decreased rest, how can the heart remain healthy and strong? In such situations *Yoga Nidra* comes as a boon.

Yoga Nidra, relaxes the body so thoroughly that half an hour of this practice has been observed to have the same effect on the system as does two hours of deep sleep. Practiced at bedtime, it not only removes all traces of stress from the body and mind but also induces sound sleep. Practicing it two-three times a day provides all the rest the heart needs to repair and rejuvenate itself completely, which can be a blessing to insomniacs.

Practicing *Tratak* before going to bed helps one get better sleep. Also, remember to exhaust your thoughts by *Swadhyaya* (self-introspection) or else they might keep coming to your mind and disturb your sleep. If you suffer from insomnia, you will do better by taking a warm bath first.

SWADHYAY

Wear loose clothing and relax in a comfortable easy chair. Close your eyes and think about the day from morning—your actions, others' actions, what you said, whether they were right, if not, what should you have said and done etc. Be honest with yourself. After finishing with your thoughts, make a noble resolve for the future. Get up and go to bed for the practice of *Yoga Nidra*.

Though a live voice is the most effective, recorded *Yoga Nidra* is more practical and gives almost the same result. This practice can be done any time provided the stomach is not full. It can also be practiced in any position, but *Shavasana* is the most relaxing.

Technique: (to be recorded and played)

- Lie down in *Shavasana* and close your eyes. Relax your body and make yourself comfortable.
- Count 50 breaths backwards. Breathing should be absolutely spontaneous. Visualise your body (for about 30 seconds). Make a resolution and repeat it three times sincerely in your mind.
- Now, run your mind over your body repeating the name of each part mentally and visualise that part.

97

- Right hand thumb: the tip – nail – first joint – second joint; index finger: tip – nail – first joint – second joint – third joint; middle finger: tip – nail – first joint – second joint– third joint; ring finger: tip – nail – first joint – second joint – third joint; palm – center of the palm – back of the hand – wrist – forearm – elbow – upper arm; shoulder – armpit; right side of the trunk – waist – right hip – right thigh knee – calf – shin – ankle – heel – sole – top of the foot; the big toe: tip – nail – first joint – second joint; second toe: tip – nail – first joint – second joint – third joint, third toe: tip – nail – first joint – second joint – third join; fourth toe: tip – nail – first joint – second joint – third joint; fifth toe: tip nail – first joint – second joint – third joint.
- Left hand thumb: (complete the left side in the same manner)
- Right shoulder blade – left shoulder blade – right side of the back – left side of the back – spine – right hip – left hip – right heel – left heel – back of the neck – back of the head – top of the head – forehead – right eyebrow – left eyebrow – right eye – left eye middle of the eyebrows – right temple

left temple – right ear – left ear – right cheek – left cheek – right nostril – left nostril – tip of the nose – upper lip – lower lip – both lips together – chin – jaw – neck – right collarbone – left collarbone – right side of the chest – left side of the chest – navel – abdomen.

- Now go into the body: teeth – tongue – throat – foodpipe – windpipe – right lung – left lung – heart – liver – stomach – small intestine – large intestine – right kidney – left kidney – bladder (add uterus and ovaries for ladies) all the bones, all the blood vessels. The brain, and all the nerves. The whole body, the whole body, the whole body (rotate your mind once or twice more over the body parts).

- Now you will visualise a few healing symbols – green meadow – snowy mountains – calm lake – white clouds – a mango tree – a white rose – torrential rain – blue sky – birds in flight – sandy bank of a wide river – a sea with massive waves – the expanding beach – starlit night – full moon and a steady candle flame.

- Visualise your heart – visualise a tiny being sitting in it and smiling at you – its eyes are full of love for you – you smile back and send lots of love to it too – you are feeling very happy.

- Remember your resolution and again repeat it three times in your mind. Be aware of your body – be aware of the room you are in – move your body – stretch it – and slowly open your eyes. The practice of *Yoga Nidra* is over.

CHAPTER TEN

Diet

have always managed to normalise essential hypertension without recommending much diet restrictions, unless the patient has high blood cholesterol. But for heart patients specially if they have high blood cholestrol, diet plays a very important role.

There are three basic types of fat in the blood – total cholesterol, high-density lipoprotein, popularly known as HDL and triglycerides. The most dangerous fat is LDL-low-density lipoprotein commonly known as bad cholesterol. Its value is determined by calculating the three basic blood fats. It is LDL, which gets deposited on the inner lining of the blood vessels, and makes them narrow and stiff - the predisposing factor for heart attacks and strokes. Triglycerides is also bad as it is thought to be a contributing factor for blood vessel damage, while HDL is labeled as good cholesterol since it acts as a scavenger and cleans up the fat deposits from arterial walls.

Cholesterol level is considered normal if it is less than 200 mg/100 mg of blood; borderline, if it is between 200 and 239/100ml, and high, when it is more than 239.

Factors responsible for high cholesterol level in blood are:

1. Heredity
2. Obesity
3. Kidney failure
4. Hypothyroidism
5. Uncontrolled diabetes
6. Some anti-hypertensive medicines.

If the cholesterol level is high due to one of the above-mentioned factors, the offending cause has to be removed. Though yoga cures these problems, many of the practices necessary for the cure, are contra-indicated in high blood pressure. Here one has to rely mainly on correct food intake to tackle the ailment. Often very simple food can yield surprisingly wonderful results.

Once a patient of mine narrated to me the story of his father whose kidneys had started to fail due to over consumption of alcohol at the tender age of fifteen. An *ayurvedic* doctor then advised him to eat some turnip daily and the gentleman followed the advice sincerely. He dried and stored turnip to consume it during the seasons when the vegetable is not available. Soon his kidneys started functioning normally and he went on to live to a ripe old age.

There are various such diet remedies for diabetes. One tablespoon of juice of fenugreek leaves taken in the morning for three months can cure early diabetes. Alternatively, one can try one tablespoon of *amla (Indian gooseberry)* juice with a cup of bitter gourd juice. *Ragi* and *guar* (Cluster beans) are also extremely beneficial for diabetes. 25 gm of *guar* cooked and eaten an hour before meals checks quick absorption of carbohydrates and maintains low blood sugar. *Ragi* is also digested and absorbed slowly.

To reduce weight, cut down on all fattening foods and increase roughage in your diet. Take cabbage and celery soup as much as possible and as many times as you want. Drink a cup of hot aniseed soup after meals. To make this soup, boil 1 tablespoon of aniseed in one glass of water for 10-15 minutes. Cabbage, celery and aniseed are said to burn stored body fat.

In case of simple high cholesterol, avoid foods, which are high in cholesterol and saturated fat. All animal fats such as butter, cream, cheese and lard are high in cholesterol, as is red meat. Vegetable oils do not contain cholesterol but some oils such as palm and coconut are considered harmful as they are saturated fats. Oils that solidify are called saturated, while the ones that remain liquid even in low temperature are called polyunsaturated fats. These oils do not increase the cholesterol level in the blood.

103

A fat that is actually beneficial to patients of high blood pressure is fish oil. It contains a polyunsaturated fat called Omega–3. This fat not only reduces blood triglyceride and increases the HDL levels; it can also prevent blood clot formation, which is the primary cause of heart attack. Omega–3 is used by the body to make cell membranes. In its absence, saturated fat is used for making them and such cell membranes are less elastic. Lack of elasticity prevents the heart from returning to a complete resting state, thereby affecting the organ adversely.

Oily fish such as tuna, sardines and salmon are high in Omega-3. It is said that eating fish five times a week can cut the risk of a stroke by half. Vegetarian foods that are rich in this fat are almonds, walnuts and avocadoes.

Foods that are known to reduce cholesterol are onion, garlic, brinjal, *chaulai*, isabgol (husk) and drumstick leaves. Ten cups of green tea a day is said to lower cholesterol considerably. Of late, a great deal of research has been done on the effects of soybean on the heart and cholesterol and it has been seen that it decreases bad cholesterol by 12% while maintaining a high HDL level. It also strengthens the heart muscles. An effective heart restorer is the bark of tree known in India as *Arjun*. The bark is soaked overnight then boiled in the morning and the water is drunk in empty stomach. Many Ayurvedic preparations are made from this ingredient. The following foods too are considered beneficial.

1. Yeast, *amla* (Indian gooseberry) and honey are said to prevent heart failure.

2. Sugarcane juice strengthens the heart.

3. Papaya with honey is a heart tonic.

4. Orange juice with honey too is a heart tonic.

5. Onion roasted on fire prevents coronary thrombosis.

6. Cloves and nutmeg are powerful blood thinners.

7. Wine, especially red one is very good for the heart. Its regular and moderate consumption has been found to reduce the risk of cardiovascular ailments by 30%.

CHAPTER ELEVEN

Oil Free and Tasty

Heart patients are forever looking for oil free food that tastes good. Here are some recipes to add to your existing menu. Half a teaspoon of olive oil can be used in each recipe.

Soya Chicken

Ingredients:

Chicken	½ kg
Onion (chopped)	½ cup
Ginger (crushed)	1 inch
Garlic (peeled)	6 cloves
Red chillies (whole)	2
Bay leaf	1
Soya sauce	2 tbs
Salt	to taste
Water	2 tbs

Method:

- Mix all the ingredients. Cover and cook till done.
- If pressure cooker is used, you will need to dry the excess water later.

Curd chicken

Ingredients:

Chicken	½ kg
Curd	½ cup
Onion (chopped)	½ cup
Garlic (chopped)	4 cloves
Green chillies (split)	2
Turmeric	a pinch
Salt	to taste

Method:

- Mix all the ingredient and cook till dry and done.

White chicken

Ingredients:

Chicken, cut into pieces	½ kg
Medium onion	1
Ginger	½ inch
Garlic	4 cloves
Coriander powder	1-½ tbs
Khuskhus (poppy seeds)	1- ½ tsp
Almonds	5
Cardamoms	2
Peppercorns	10
Curd	¼ cup
Water	¼ cup
Salt	to taste

Method:

- Grind onion, ginger, garlic to a paste and mix it with chicken. Add curd, water and salt and cook it on slow fire till done and dry. Add ½ cup water and bring it to a boil, then reduce the fire.

109

- Grind blanched almonds and *khuskhus*. Add to the chicken.
- Simmer for 4 – 5 minutes.
- Remove from fire.

Mustard fish

Ingredients:

Any non-oily fish	5 pieces
Mustard seeds	2 tbs
Garlic	4 cloves
Green chili	1
Turmeric	¼ tbs
Salt	to taste
Water	2-3 tbs
Mustard oil	A few drops

Method:

- Mix everything together except the oil, in a thick bottomed pot and put it on fire till done.
- Sprinkle the oil on top and remove from fire.

CURD FISH

Ingredients:

Any non-oily fish	4 pieces
Onion chopped	1 tbs
Garlic (chopped)	2-3 cloves
Green cardamom (split)	1
Bay leaf (split)	1
Salt	to taste
Chili powder	a pinch

Method:

- Mix every thing in a thick bottom pot, cover it and cook till done.

TOMATO FISH

Ingredients:

Non-oily fish	4 pieces
Medium Tomato (cut into pieces)	1
Garlic (chopped)	3 cloves
Green chili (halved lengthwise)	1
Mustard seeds (ground)	½ tsp
Salt	to taste
Water	¼ cup

Method:

- Mix everything in a thick bottomed pot, cover and put it on low fire till done.

111

MUSTARD MUSHROOM

Ingredients:

Mushroom	100 grams
Mustard seeds	1-½ tbs
Garlic	4 cloves
Water	2-3 tbs
Green chili	½
Turmeric powder	⅛ tsp
Salt	to taste

Method:

- Cut mushroom into small pieces.
- Grind mustard, garlic and chili to a paste.
- Mix everything and cook it till done and dry (pressure cooker can be used).

ONION MUSHROOM

Ingredients:

Mushroom	100 grams
Onion (chopped)	2 tbs
Garlic (chopped)	4 cloves
Ginger (chopped)	½ inch

Pepper (crushed)	1 pinch
Turmeric	1 pinch
Water	1 tbs
Salt to taste	

Method:

- Mix everything and pressure cook till done. Dry up remaining water.

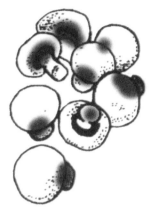

Veg Bhurta

Ingredients:

Brinjal	1
Potato	1
Tomato	1
Green chili (chopped)	1
Coriander leaves (chopped)	to taste
Salt	to taste
Mustard oil	a few drops

Method:

- Roast brinjal on fire till soft.
- Remove from fire, and remove the charred skin.
- Roast the tomato too and remove its skin.
- Boil the potato and peel.
- Mash the three vegetables.
- Mix everything together.

CAULIFLOWER MASALA

Ingredients:

Medium cauliflower	1
Tomatoes	2
Medium onions	3
Medium potatoes	2
Bay leaf	1
Cinnamon stick	½
Ginger	½ inch
Cloves garlic	5
Turmeric	a pinch
Salt	to taste

Method:

- Grind 1 onion, ginger and garlic to a fine paste and rub it into the whole cauliflower.

- Peel potatoes and onions.

- Mix the whole vegetable and the rest of the ingredients in a pressure cooker. Cover without putting the weight and put it on low fire till the vegetables leave water. If there is not enough water, add half a cup of water and pressure cook it till done. Later the water should be dried up in an open pan.

Mustard Cabbage

Ingredients:

Shredded cabbage	1 cup
Mustard seeds	1 tbs
Garlic (peeled)	2 cloves
Green chili	½
Tomato medium	½
Turmeric	a pinch
Water	2 tbs
Salt	to taste
Mustard oil	a few drops

Method:

- Grind mustard, garlic and chilli.
- Mix everything except the oil in a thick bottomed pot and cook it on low fire till done. Add the oil and remove from fire.

Cumin peas

Ingredients:

Peas (shelled)	1 cup
Milk	2 tbs
Cumin seeds	1 tbs
Dry red chilli	½
Salt	to taste

Method:

- Cook the peas and mash it. Mix milk and salt well into it.

115

Bamboo Shoots with Vegetables

Ingredients:

Potato	1
Brinjal	½
Pumpkin	150 gms
Lady's finger	2
Bamboo shoots	2-3 pieces
Water	1 cup
Gram flour	1 tbs
Turmeric powder	¼ tbs
Mustard seeds	¼ tbs
Fenugreek seeds	¼ tbs
Mustard oil	¼ tbs
Curry leaves	10-12

Method:

- Cut potato, pumpkin and brinjal into big pieces. Cut off the ends of the lady's fingers.
- Pressure cook all the vegetables (except lady's fingers), turmeric, salt and water till done.
- Add lady's fingers.

- Mix curd and gram flour with 2-3 tablespoons of water and pour over the vegetable and simmer for 5 minutes.
- Remove from fire.
- In a big spoon heat the oil. When it starts to smoke, add mustard and fenugreek seeds.
- When the seeds start to crackle, add curry leaves and chilli. And then pour this over the vegetable.

117

CHAPTER TWELVE

Avoidable Evils

After a heart attack, the heart can never be the same again. It remains vulnerable for life because the tissues, that have died, are lost forever: they do not regenerate. Hence, utmost care should be taken to protect this vital organ from all potential dangers so as not to invite another attack.

■ Negative thoughts

Nature never lets the mind be empty. Thoughts of various kinds plague it incessantly. Most of these thoughts are negative in nature such as thoughts of worries, fear and anger. These thoughts are known to weaken the system by actually destroying body cells including those of the heart.

119

Furthermore, negative thoughts cause the release of neuropeptides, which oxidize the LDL. And for a heart patient it can prove lethal, especially after a heart attack, when the person's mind is already filled with shock, resentment and depression.

To learn not to entertain negative thoughts, make a sincere effort to make your mind positive by repeating often "**I am a positive person, I always think positive**". Positive thoughts cause the release of nitric oxide in the blood. This chemical has a healing power.

■ Bottling up

Often heart patients think that expressing their fears and anxiety will reveal their weakness and invoke pity in the listener. They bottle up their emotions and try to put up a brave front. This can harm the heart. It is advisable to find a sympathetic friend or relative and pour out one's agony. In the absence of such a person one should write down one's feelings in details – it is an easy but effective device for releasing one's pent up emotions. Confession, as practiced in churches is very therapeutic.

■ Lack of Exercise

Not exercising adequately can further weaken the heart while exercise causes new blood pathways to develop, and so, if one artery closes down, others are there to nourish your body tissues.

▪ Incorrect breathing

Shallow breathing deprives the system of the much-needed oxygen while fast breathing floods the blood with too much oxygen too quickly that can make one feel dizzy. Slow and deep breathing is the best, not only because the oxygen is utilized better, but also because it induces deep relaxation. Concentration on one's breaths as done in yogic abdominal breathing successfully diverts the mind from unnecessary and damaging thoughts.

▪ Lack of Rest

Nothing should be done in excess, including physical activities. The heart needs rest from time to time. So, instead of spending your energy by continuous activities, for which the heart has to make extra effort, one should take a short nap now and again. Alternatively you can practice short *Yoga Nidra* of 5 or 10 minutes duration at any time during the day.

▪ Fast pulse

If the heart beats more than its healthy limit, it can get strained. Even if it beats ten to twelve times more in a miniute, it has to beat 27,000 times more in a day. Slow and deep *Ujjayi Pranayam* slows down the pulse almost instantaneously, so also breathing in a 1:2 ratio i.e the exhalation is double the ratio as to the inhalation.

121

▥ Boredom

Boredom is detrimental to one's health. Give no chance to the mind to get bored and get depressed over the ailment. Rather, engage in as many de-stressing activities as possible. These include listening to music, dancing, drumming, gardening, painting, playing, praying, shopping and stargazing. Some housewives find household chores such as dish washing extremely relaxing.

▥ Drugs that enhance sexual potency

Most of these drugs encourage platelet clumping which can lead to cardiac arrest and death.

▥ Scary movies

Violent movies make the heart race wildly. It has been observed that the pulse rate during such movies is never below 90 per minute and during very fearful scenes it can be go as high as 150 beats which can be dangerous for the heart's health. Hence heart patients should stay away from them.

▥ Sun

Avoid over exposure to the sun and other forms of heat if you are on strong anti-hypertension drug. It can cause the blood pressure to fall very low resulting in a blackout.

▥ Cold bath

Cold constricts blood vessels pushing the blood pressure up. If

you suffer from a malignant type of high blood pressure, cold bath can raise the blood pressure to a dangerous height.

◼ Driving

Avoid driving unless it is absolutely necessary. Remember that one day behind a wheel is more strenuous than a full day's hard work.

◼ Heavy meals

A heavy meal takes longer to digest which means the stomach needs more blood for a much longer duration, and the heart works that much more to maintain the blood supply. It puts an unnecessary load on the heart. It can be avoided by taking smaller and lighter meals, which can be digested in a couple of hours. Also avoid late dinner as food eaten late at night not only uses much of our reserve energy, it has less chances of getting digested properly leading to gas formation which can push against the heart and cause much discomfort.

◼ Coffee

Caffeine in coffee is an extremely strong stimulant, which can increase palpitation. If that is the case with you, avoid coffee, as slow pulse is healthier for the heart.

◼ Betel nut

It is known to constrict the bronchi, which is dangerous for the heart.

123

■ Humidity

Humidity increases the risk of getting an attack especially in the elderly.

■ Anti-Cholesterol Drug

Most anti-cholesterol drugs block absorption of fat soluble vitamins which are Vitamin A, D, E and K. In a research in the west, the common drug Mevacor seemed to produce cancer in animals.

■ Gossip

Lastly, avoid gossiping as it has been seen to cause heart problems.

CHAPTER THIRTEEN

Strengthening the Heart

Just the thought of pickles can make the mouth salivate and reading about a haunted house can give most people goose bumps such is the power of words on our body via the mind. 'Tension', 'inflation', 'competition', 'deadline', 'stress', 'income-tax', 'raid', 'murder', 'dacoits', 'heart attack', 'high blood pressure', are some of the constantly used words in our daily life, which are bound to affect our system in a negative way. Looking at dreary files and depressing bills the whole daylong can only make matters worse and one cannot wish them away either. They are realities we have to face. One can only counter their effects and a very effective method is to reflect on positive life giving words. Looking at green colour and some healing

127

objects also helps. Green colour is seen to have a calming effect on the nervous system. Here is a simple exercise that combines them all which can do wonders to your heart in the shortest possible time. Choose one or more words from the following list. Look at one of the pictures given in the following pages and taking slow breaths, mentally repeat the words for a few minutes. You can do it as often as you want. Alternatively, read the entire list, reflecting on each word for a few seconds and then stare at each picture, again for a few seconds.

List of words to read:

Oum

Ananda

Peace

Tranquility

Happiness

Laughter

Relax

Cheerful

Smile

Merry

Mirth

Sunshine

Joy

Purity

Devotion

Kindness

Love

Compassion

Like

Affection

Rejuvenation

Space

Innocence

Beauty

Soothing

Bliss

Blessing

God

Grace

Guru

Fairy

Angel

Miracle

Sympathy

Friend

Genuine

Gem

Shoonya

Shanti

Pictures to look at:

In the end, keep faith, faith is a great healer. Pray, repeat the Lord's name, chant *mantras*, sing devotional songs, do whatever you like to remain connected with the Divine as long as possible. Remember to be thankful for everything. Your heart will be happy and healthy.

REFERENCES

1. Dr. Michael Sharon, *Nutrients A to Z*, Rupa & Co.

2. Dr. Aman, *Medicinal Secrets of Your Food*.

3. J. D. Ritcliff, *I am Joe's Body*, Berkley Publishing Group, New York.

4. *Mayo Clinic Family Health Book*, Willima Morrow & Company, Inc., New York.

5. Swami Sivananda, *Japa Yoga*, Divine Life Society.

6. Swami Sivananda, *Mind – Its Mysteries and Control*, Divine Life Society.

7. Swami Sivananda, *Sure Ways for Success in Life & God Realization*, Divine Life Society.

8. Swami Sivananda, *Concentration and Meditation*, Divine Life Society.

9. *Hatha Yoga Pradipika*, Bihar School of Yoga, Munger.

10. Swami Satyananda Saraswati, *Asana Pranayama Mudra Bandha*, Bihar School of Yoga, Munger.

11. Swami Satyananda Saraswati, *Yoga Nidra*, Bihar School of Yoga, Munger.

12. Swami Satyananda Saraswati, *Meditation from Tantra*, Bihar School of Yoga, Munger.

13. Swami Satyananda Saraswati, *Self Realisation*, Bihar School of Yoga, Munger.

14. Swami Satyananda Saraswati, *Yogic Cure for Common Diseases*, Bihar School of Yoga, Munger.

15. *The Effect of Yoga on Hypertension*, Bihar School of Yoga, Munger.

INDEX

Printed in Poland
by Amazon Fulfillment
Poland Sp. z o.o., Wrocław